FOCUS ON MEDIA BIAS

FAKE NEWS IN FOCUS

by Alex Gatling

FOCUS
READERS.

VOYAGER

www.focusreaders.com

Focus Readers is distributed by North Star Editions:
sales@northstareditions.com | 888-417-0195

Produced for Focus Readers by Red Line Editorial.

Photographs ©: Shutterstock Images, cover (left), cover (right), 1 (left), 1 (right), 7, 8–9, 11, 12–13, 17, 18–19, 21, 26–27, 29, 32–33, 37, 43; Jose Luis Magana/AP Images, 4–5; Library of Congress, 15; David Goldman/AP Images, 23; Susan Walsh/AP Images, 25; Chris Pizzello/AP Images, 31; Red Line Editorial, 35, 45; Ty O'Neil/SOPA Images/Sipa USA/AP Images, 38–39; CNP/AdMedia/SIPA/Newscom, 41

Library of Congress Cataloging-in-Publication Data
Names: Gatling, Alex, author.
Title: Fake news in focus / Alex Gatling.
Description: Lake Elmo : Focus Readers, 2022. | Series: Focus on media bias | Includes index. | Audience: Grades 4-6
Identifiers: LCCN 2021005874 (print) | LCCN 2021005875 (ebook) | ISBN 9781644938652 (hardcover) | ISBN 9781644939116 (paperback) | ISBN 9781644939574 (ebook) | ISBN 9781644939970 (pdf)
Subjects: LCSH: Media literacy--United States--Juvenile literature. | Fake news--United States--Juvenile literature.
Classification: LCC P96.M42 U5845 2022 (print) | LCC P96.M42 (ebook) | DDC 302.23/1--dc23
LC record available at https://lccn.loc.gov/2021005874
LC ebook record available at https://lccn.loc.gov/2021005875

Printed in the United States of America
Mankato, MN
082021

ABOUT THE AUTHOR

Alex Gatling is a children's book writer from Texas. She enjoys traveling, learning about science and history, and staying informed on current events.

TABLE OF CONTENTS

CHAPTER 1

FAKE NEWS, REAL CONSEQUENCES

In 2016, an article quickly spread online. It claimed that top politicians were harming children at a pizza restaurant in Washington, DC. The article said the politicians kidnapped children. It said they sold the children into slavery from the restaurant's basement. The article was completely made-up. There was no child abuse happening in the restaurant. The restaurant did not even have a basement.

Fake news caused some people to believe that serious crimes were taking place at Comet Ping Pong, a pizza restaurant.

Even so, some people believed the article. The restaurant owner received death threats. One man went to check the restaurant himself. He walked in with two guns and fired shots. Fortunately, no one was hurt or killed. But other cases of fake news have resulted in death.

The modern use of the phrase "fake news" began during the 2016 US presidential election. Some website owners created and spread false information for money. Researchers studying this activity used the phrase "fake news." But the phrase's usage has shifted over time. Some politicians began using it to harm the reputation of legitimate **news media**. Also, certain news outlets used the phrase as a way to raise people's interest in articles.

Many people have described fake news as a crisis. Fake news has led to some very real

President Donald Trump often used the term "fake news" to describe reporting that he didn't like.

consequences. But the issue is complicated. **Disinformation** has a long history. People use the phrase "fake news" in different ways. And many people have lost trust in **established** news media. All these factors make it important to clearly define fake news. Only then can we see how big the problem really is.

CHAPTER 2

DEFINING FAKE NEWS

Fake news is a type of disinformation. Disinformation includes articles and videos designed to trick people. For example, it might show facts out of context. Without context, the facts seem to support a certain view. Or disinformation might give only the facts that support one viewpoint. It can also involve language that makes people upset. The language uses people's emotions to change their opinions.

Fake news tends to use language that makes people angry or afraid.

Fake news has three key parts. First, the information is false. Second, it is created intentionally. Third, it is presented in a way to make it seem like factual news. Fake news fools people by looking like real reporting.

Established news media follow standards to make sure information is factual. These standards include using reliable sources and **objective** language. Fake news does not follow standards. But it tricks people into thinking it does.

Sometimes real reporters make mistakes. They may get facts wrong. Or their sources may prove untrustworthy. But this is not fake news. The mistakes were not intentional. The reporters did

➤ THINK ABOUT IT

Why would reliable sources and objective language help ensure that information is factual?

▲ Reporters record their interviews to make sure they use accurate quotes.

not mean to deceive people. Often, they post corrections when they get something wrong.

Some researchers argue that people overuse the phrase "fake news." They say people should use the phrase more carefully. Otherwise, fake news might seem like a bigger problem than it really is. For these researchers, fake news is simply a new form of disinformation. And people have been spreading disinformation for many years.

CHAPTER 3

DISINFORMATION THEN

Disinformation has been around for centuries. In the 1100s, false stories were spread to increase hatred of Jewish people in Europe. In the 1700s, disinformation encouraged racism against Indigenous peoples in the American colonies. And in the 1800s, false stories led to violence against enslaved Black people.

Until the late 1800s, the news media was made up of highly **partisan** newspapers. Writers often

Some enslaved Black people faced horrible violence after false stories accused them of crimes.

insulted politicians. They also changed facts to support their views.

The 1830s saw the beginning of the penny presses. These cheap newspapers used exciting or shocking language. And they didn't worry much about accuracy. For example, one story claimed there were aliens on the moon. The story was completely made-up. But the "Great Moon Hoax" of 1835 sold lots of papers.

Disinformation continued through the 1800s. In the 1890s, rival newspapers competed for readers. They engaged in a practice known as yellow journalism. The papers reported rumors as if they were facts. And they used shocking headlines to grab people's attention. News reporting, opinions, and fiction all mixed together.

In the early 1900s, more people began seeking objectivity and facts in reporting. Objective

In 1835, a newspaper in New York published a drawing showing creatures living on the moon.

reporting proved to be a good business model. Newspapers were successful even without shocking headlines.

Reporters started to consider the ethics of their work. The Society of Professional Journalists created its first code of ethics in 1926. This group has updated its code over the years. Many newspapers also formed guidelines for reporters.

One common standard is verifying information before sharing it. Another standard is providing context for facts. That way, readers get the full and complete story. A third standard says reporters should correct their errors. And a fourth says reporters should be impartial. This means they should treat all views equally instead of taking a side.

Disinformation still exists. But established news media are typically not the ones spreading it. Because of the internet, information flows differently now. Before the internet was widely used, the news media determined what

> **THINK ABOUT IT**

How do you know if something is fiction or fact? How can you tell the difference between made-up stories and real reporting?

▲ Today, most people recognize tabloids as untrustworthy news sources.

information went out. Now, technology has made it easy for anyone to spread information on social media. People can quickly post and share articles. They can share both real news and fake news. And fake news often gets views by imitating real news.

CHAPTER 4

FAKE NEWS NOW

Creators of fake news usually have one of two goals. They either want to influence people's beliefs, or they want to make money. For example, teenagers in Eastern Europe spread fake news during the 2016 US presidential election. They didn't care who won the election. They just wanted to make money.

Regardless of their goals, all fake-news creators go through a similar process. First,

During the 2016 election, fake news spread faster on Facebook than on any other social media site.

creators get a website. They choose the web address carefully. They want it to seem as if it's an established news site. For example, abcnews.go.com is an established news site. However, abcnews.com.co was a fake-news site.

Next, creators get content. Some make up their own fake stories. Others copy and paste from **satire** websites. Creators try to make the stories seem factual. Then they use clickbait to get attention. Clickbait uses shocking headlines that link back to the creators' websites. The goal is to make people click on the links. This is how creators make money. They sell space on their websites to advertising companies. Each new click to a website earns money for its creator.

Finally, creators use social media to spread their fake news. For example, creators post links to their websites in Facebook groups. They find

▲ People with low levels of trust in established news outlets are more likely to spread fake news.

groups that will likely be interested in their links. They hope people will visit their websites.

Some people recognize fake news when they see it. They don't click on the links. But other people do believe fake news. This can be because of their **biases**. Everyone has beliefs that shape how they view new information. These beliefs can cause mistakes in people's thinking.

For instance, people sometimes share articles without reading them. They only look at the headlines and then form an opinion. Also, people are more likely to trust information that supports what they already believe. This is called confirmation bias. It leads people to trust fake news that confirms their views.

Social media algorithms support this type of bias. Algorithms are instructions for computers. They determine what people see on social media sites. Algorithms collect data on users. For instance, algorithms know which articles users share. They also know when users comment. Over time, algorithms learn users' interests. Then the

> **THINK ABOUT IT**

What are the pros and cons of using algorithms to control what people see on social media?

▲ In 2017, a left-leaning article falsely claimed that police burned the camps of people protesting an oil pipeline.

algorithms fill each user's social media page with content that the user will find interesting.

Most fake news is spread by people on the political extremes. Overall, Republicans on the far right share more fake news than any other group. However, Democrats on the far left share fake news, too. In the late 2010s, for example, many Democrats shared fake stories about President Donald Trump.

WEAPONIZING THE TERM

Politicians don't always like what news articles say about them. That doesn't make the news articles false. But some politicians still refer to those articles as fake news.

For example, the news network CNN released a story in January 2017. The story said Russian agents had damaging information about president-elect Donald Trump. According to the news story, Trump knew they had it. However, Trump denied knowing about it. He said the story was false.

CNN stood by the story's accuracy. The network challenged Trump to say what was false about the story. Later in the week, Trump held a press conference. A reporter from CNN tried to ask him a question. Trump refused to answer.

△ The White House hosts press conferences so that reporters can ask questions of political leaders.

He called the reporter "fake news." And he later called the press the "enemy of the people."

After Trump took office, the White House banned certain news outlets from some events. The US Constitution protects freedom of the press. That means the government cannot **censor** news media. Trump's team argued the president was fighting against biased media reports. But media experts worried he was reducing press freedom.

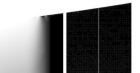

CHAPTER 5

A FAKE-NEWS CRISIS?

According to a 2019 poll, Americans saw "made-up news" as a serious problem. They saw it as a bigger problem than terrorism or illegal immigration. They found it about as problematic as violent crime and climate change. Only drug addiction and health-care costs concerned Americans more. Most Americans said made-up news affected their trust in the government. They blamed politicians the most.

Many US citizens say fake news has decreased their faith in government.

However, there was a problem with the poll. The term "made-up news" was not clearly defined. As a result, it's not clear what Americans meant when they responded. They might have been talking about fake news. If so, Americans' concern was an overreaction. Research shows that only a small minority of Americans actually see fake news. Even fewer people share it. This was true even during the 2016 election, when the fake-news issue began.

Fake news is spread through social media. However, less than 20 percent of Americans said they got political news from social media. And most of those people said they expected that news to be false.

According to the poll, more than 60 percent of Republicans said made-up news was a serious problem. Only 40 percent of Democrats felt the

▲ Republicans tend to have less trust in established media outlets than Democrats do.

same. This difference suggests the two groups were not defining "made-up news" in the same way. Also, Republicans were three times more likely to blame reporters for made-up news. Nearly 60 percent of Republicans said reporters create a lot of made-up news. So, Republicans might not have defined "made-up news" as fake news. Instead, they might have been talking about bias in established news media.

In the poll, people said they responded to made-up news in different ways. Some said they fact-checked the news themselves. Others said they dropped news sources entirely. But it was unclear which news sources people were dropping. They may have been dropping fake-news websites. Or they may have been dropping established news sources. People might have heard politicians describe established sources as fake news. Or they might have disliked what established sources said. Because of confirmation bias, people tend to choose news sources that agree with their views. They also tend to avoid sources that disagree with

> **THINK ABOUT IT**

What are the benefits of reading news stories you don't agree with?

▲ Rachel Maddow of MSNBC offers a Democratic perspective. As a result, few Republicans watch her show.

their views. However, that doesn't make those sources wrong.

This data suggests the actual crisis might not be fake news. Instead, the crisis might be a loss of trust in established news media. Research confirms that fake news decreases trust in news media. But a lack of trust in the media is not new.

CHAPTER 6

BIAS IN THE MEDIA

In a 2020 poll, Americans said news media should keep them informed. They also said the media should provide accurate and fair reports. In addition, they said the media should hold politicians **accountable**. However, many Americans did not think the news media performed these jobs successfully.

Trust in the media has been falling for several decades. Since 1972, a polling company has

In 2020, only 9 percent of Americans had a high level of trust in the news media.

asked Americans about their trust in news media. Trust was at its highest point in 1976. At that time, reporters had investigated key issues. Americans generally admired their work.

After that, trust in the media started falling. The lowest point was in 2016. Only 32 percent of Americans trusted the news media's accuracy and fairness. There was a big difference between Democrats and Republicans. More than half of Democrats said they trusted news media. Only 14 percent of Republicans did.

Many people have accused the media of bias. However, they disagree on how the media shows bias. Researchers studied how Democrats and Republicans viewed the same news articles. On both sides, when people saw articles that supported their own party, they said the articles were unbiased. Meanwhile, when people saw articles that favored the other party, they said the articles were biased. So, people tended to see the news as biased when it didn't agree with their own views.

WHICH NEWS OUTLETS DO AMERICANS TRUST? ◁

Different news outlets attract different audiences. This chart shows which news media are most trusted by Democrats and Republicans.

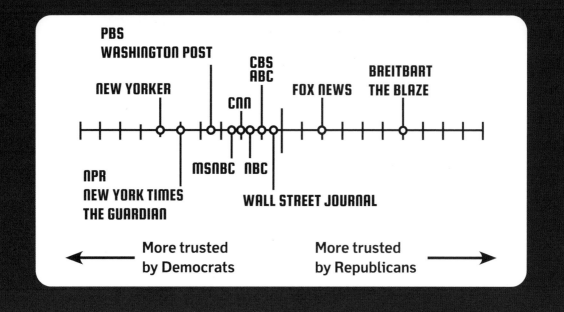

Also, the media includes thousands of news outlets. They all give different perspectives on the same events. Reporters might show bias in how they share information. But this is part of having a free press. People can choose which media to get their news from. And they can consume multiple media sources to get multiple views.

Researchers have recognized one bias in the media. It involves what the media consider newsworthy. Studies have found that media outlets are biased toward topics that will get people's attention. Without readers or viewers, media outlets would not exist. So, they report on high-interest or dramatic stories. Other topics might be more important but less dramatic. Those topics tend to get less media coverage.

Bias can certainly exist in the media. But that does not make it fake news or disinformation. The

▲ Having many news sources to choose from is one benefit of a free press.

intention is not to deceive. Many established news media follow codes of ethics. These standards include objectivity. Even so, some researchers argue that objectivity can sometimes lead to unwanted outcomes. In certain cases, a desire for objectivity can contribute to the spread of disinformation.

CHAPTER 7

DISINFORMATION AND THE MEDIA TODAY

Research shows that **election fraud** is extremely rare in the United States. Even so, millions of Americans feared it during and after the 2020 presidential election. People didn't get this idea from fake-news websites. Instead, many got it from established news media.

Researchers studied this spread. They found that several conservative politicians had talked about election fraud. Then news media shared

Many voters believed the 2020 election involved massive fraud. However, there was no evidence to support this claim.

that idea with the general public. Three reporting standards led news media to do so. The first standard is that reporters focus on politicians. If a politician says something, it's news. Second, reporters want attention-grabbing headlines. Third, reporters want to seem objective.

The first two standards sometimes bring attention to false ideas. For example, suppose a politician makes a claim. It might be true or false. Most reporters want to report on the claim right away. But by reporting quickly, the reporters share the claim without verifying it. Reporters could wait to share their report until after checking the claim. But they might lose people's attention to reporters who shared the story earlier. Also, the third standard means reporters might not call false claims "disinformation." They might worry about appearing to be biased if they do so.

In 2020, the media reported heavily on Senator Ted Cruz and others who made unproven claims of election fraud.

Researchers say these standards helped disinformation spread in 2020. When politicians spoke falsely about election fraud, many news outlets wanted to seem objective and unbiased. So, they simply reported what the politicians said. Millions of people came to believe election fraud was a serious issue, even though it wasn't.

It's possible to report disinformation without spreading it. Reporters can start their articles with facts. Then they can report on a politician's claim. They can end by fact-checking that claim. In 2020, more reporters began doing this.

Social media websites also started labeling misleading claims. Both Twitter and Facebook added these warnings. Some users liked the changes. Others said these changes were biased against certain views.

The issue is complicated for news outlets. It's also complicated for people who just want to know the truth. Many media experts say we are in a post-truth era. Public opinion is shaped more by feelings and personal beliefs than by objective facts. But there have always been people spreading disinformation. And many have done so to sway public opinion.

Tweet

Donald J. Trump
@realDonaldTrump

Some or all of the content shared in this Tw
is disputed and might be misleading about an
election or other civic process. Learn more

STOP THE FRAUD!

...arn about US 2020 election s...

▲ In 2021, Twitter banned Donald Trump for making false claims that led to violence.

Other media experts argue we are in a post-*trust* era. After all, many Americans doubt what politicians say. And they ignore real news from established news media. But this lack of trust is also not new. And it isn't necessarily a bad thing. It's an opportunity for people to develop their skills. People can learn how to check facts and think critically. They can learn how to tell real news from fake news.

STOPPING THE SPREAD

You can help stop the spread of disinformation. Start by checking the date on the article. Look for current information rather than stories from years ago. Also, be sure to read more than just the headline. Make sure the article's information matches the headline. Notice how you feel as you read the article. Writers of disinformation often try to make readers angry or scared. If you feel a strong emotion, pause. Take time to investigate the article further.

Check the article for signs of bias. Does the writer seem to have an opinion? If so, he or she might not be giving the full story. Similarly, check the article for context. Disinformation will often focus on one key fact. More-objective writing will put that fact into context.

Objective News Report	Disinformation
Shares how the information might be limited	Claims to be absolutely true and certain
Describes multiple views accurately and in a respectful way	Insults certain people or views, or describes only one view
Uses neutral language	Appeals to people's emotions
Puts information into context	Presents information out of context

When in doubt, verify the information in an article. See if the writer included sources. Be doubtful about stories that don't provide sources.

Finally, notice what you believe and think. Then challenge yourself to read from other points of view. This will help you avoid confirmation bias. Remember that disagreeing with something does not make it false.

FOCUS ON
FAKE NEWS

Write your answers on a separate piece of paper.

1. Write a paragraph explaining the main ideas of Chapter 5.

2. Why do you think people believe fake news and other forms of disinformation?

3. Which of the following is not a standard in professional journalism's code of ethics?

> **A.** using impartial language to treat all views equally
> **B.** providing context for the facts
> **C.** sharing information before verifying it

4. What could be one reason that trust in the media dropped to its lowest point in 2016?

> **A.** Reporters had investigated key issues that Americans cared about.
> **B.** Fake news spread around the US presidential election.
> **C.** The Society of Professional Journalists updated its code of ethics.

Answer key on page 48.

GLOSSARY

accountable
Responsible, or expected to give good reasons for one's actions and decisions.

biases
Attitudes that cause people to treat certain ideas unfairly.

censor
To force people not to write or publish about certain topics.

disinformation
False information that is intentionally spread to deceive people, often to influence public opinion.

election fraud
The crime of interfering with an election, either by adding or taking away votes, to change the election's result.

established
Accepted by many people and existing for a long period of time.

news media
Forms of mass media that deliver news to the public. They include print newspapers and magazines, online newspapers and magazines, TV news stations, and radio stations.

objective
Showing facts rather than opinions.

partisan
Biased in favor of a particular group, usually a political group.

satire
Fictional writing that uses humor to comment on real-life people and events.

TO LEARN MORE

BOOKS

Dell, Pamela. *Understanding the News*. North Mankato, MN: Capstone Press, 2019.

Harris, Duchess. *The Fake News Phenomenon*. Minneapolis: Abdo Publishing, 2018.

Harris, Duchess, with Laura K. Murray. *Uncovering Bias in the News*. Minneapolis: Abdo Publishing, 2018.

NOTE TO EDUCATORS

Visit **www.focusreaders.com** to find lesson plans, activities, links, and other resources related to this title.

INDEX

Answer Key: 1. Answers will vary; **2.** Answers will vary; **3.** C; **4.** B